BLACK ROSE
WILTED

FREDERICK JONES

BLACK ROSE
WILTED

TATE PUBLISHING
AND **ENTERPRISES**, LLC

Published by Tate Publishing & Enterprises, LLC
127 E. Trade Center Terrace | Mustang, Oklahoma 73064 USA
1.888.361.9473 | www.tatepublishing.com

Tate Publishing is committed to excellence in the publishing industry. The company reflects the philosophy established by the founders, based on Psalm 68:11,
"The Lord gave the word and great was the company of those who published it."

Published in the United States of America

ISBN: 978-1-63063-727-9
Poetry / Subjects & Themes / Love
14.11.21

Contents

911

Maybe exoneration is warranted;
maybe, it is not!
My only job is to have the nations' foes rot
The deeds of evil of which they perform.
Surely, death is earned to them.
Killing the innocent for a "statement" our enemies do
So eloquently!
Call to 911 thousands strew.
Can we recall 9/11?
See the irony here?
But still, I am merely doing my duty,
A hero I am not,
Only a selfless servant to our great nation.
Heroes are the brethren who have gave all
So that I have the liberty to write about the sensations of
    which I feel the calling.
The thank-you is warming.
They calm the storm that brews so heavily within.
So I say to you, America,
Thank you.

Anubis

The wicked ways
Of which thee
Strays
More radioactive
Than the rays thrown
From Ra
Like the constant flow of water
Through a straw
Contagious it is
To rush toward
Anubis

As the Ghosts Say

Sitting here with the ghosts that say,
"She will never once
shine her rays your way."
I discredit them constantly.
As I see our talks
increase swiftly
with long walks for several days
now my state of being stuck in this daze
to hear your voice at which time I will truly fall
with the unexpected response of
"We'll see."
To this devoted declaration,
my heart now devoured
like brie and blood red wine
for all these decades,
three decades to be quite precise.
It was always you that did entice.
Entice my heart, my soul.
I only need you for this breathing body
to be whole.
Otherwise, I am only
A zombie
with no purpose on this earth
but to simply,

and miserably,
decompose until all of my body has left me.
Without you in my life,
there is no life,
just breath
with no thought.
Don't leave me.
don't leave,
why are you leaving me?

Asunder

Indecisive she remains.
I am falling for her
deeply into asunder. I plummet
face first.
How is it that we may talk for hours
and text for days,
then without warning,
she disappears.
I text, no response.
I call, no answer.
Late at night,
then,
my phone rings.
Happy I am that she calls,
forgiving all her ignoring
again.
Is she going to call me sweetie again tonight?
My plight flies above all heights
when she calls me sweetie.
Suddenly, she has done no wrong
now.
The next day is here,
and no text or call saying, "Hi, sweetie"
Is this the beginning of the end?

We never really started,
as the first person-to-person was slightly thwarted!
So now I ask myself,
"Is it me?
Is it her?"
I spent my heart on her,
and now my heart claims to be bankrupt.
May the deities
bless and save me from inevitable and everlasting
    depression
from this emotional recession.

Atomic Fumes

This illness
consumes
like heavy atomic fumes
devouring every molecule
of what I define as pure ridicule.
Why!
I loved her with all my heart.
These voices empower
like the birds of the twin towers.
Innocence made to cower.
Pestilence took over and moves forward.
I am no longer me,
out of control of thoughts and actions.
My imagination
has occupied my operations,
physically,
mentally.
I am not me!
What has happened!
What have I now done?
Help!

Aura

The hours you keep are quite steep.
Staring at me from the door as I sleep,
how silently you enter deep into the night.
With eyes closed, you are in my sight,
feeling your aura,
sensing Great Pandora.
It is you of who my mind wanders.
Every minute of the nocturnal hours
are spent in squander,
praying for your return.
It is your heart I yearn.
For without you,
On a great pyre may I burn

Bat Wings

The bats flicker their wings as they swarm the skies
of September's evening air.
Flying above the blue water, I lay sulking in.
Have I sinned?
Somehow, with this sight, I have found a grin.
For as alleged sins, I may be prosecuted
from a judge not solicited.
Freedom is on my mind.
Evil dictation is no longer
the survival sign.
Your love once benign
now as malignant
and stagnant as cancer.
Thank you, though,
for giving me the eternally saving
answer, prematurely.
Save me from your suffering.
I have spent years buffering
minus your abuse.
I would gladly remain to amuse you,
but you are more amused
with your booze
than me as your muse.
Why do I waste my time

with you? It's love you lack
love, you lack.
And all you stand for is *six six six*.
I sacrifice to you my heart.
In the night, I am merely theft by taking.
Could you at least spare mercy on me?
Who has forever forsaken
eternal my love be?
No matter how morbid
your eyes see,
pray for you I may
even as your dagger slay.
I am merely bait
for you
as I impatiently wait
in this unlit room.
Only for you.
Answer me!
Answer me!
Alone I sit here waiting for thee.
Answer me!

Battle Clouds

I look upon the sky.
God, I wish I could fly.
I see the formation of clouds
marching straight south
to flaming shrouds
from her dragon mouth.
The storm brews
as I hear the vampire
cry for red booze
with life force drained
and relationships sprained.
Eternally, I am refrained.
My thoughts matter not,
forever retained in my heart
and mind.
Your touch on my skin,
so kind.
As my weakness strengthens,
every rational part of me goes blind.
How can you do this to me?
With one look,
one smile, crooked in nature
one touch of the lips,
I'm forever enslaved.

Cloud of the night forest,
with your cunning embrace,
may we now end this chase?

Blessed Nightmare

this dream finally
is reality.
all these years
suffering and sacrificing,
now, my sweet dream stands before me
as real as the bumpy chill that crawls upon this skin.
once only a dream,
my blessed nightmare
now gives me fear.
forward, though, I march.
fail I will not.
my blessed nightmare,
this sin I bare.
my blessed nightmare,
how sweet your lips upon mine.
impatiently, I have waited.
now, my time has come.
this now is my fare to prevail.
my blessed nightmare,
into the deep blue, we gracefully sail.

Brother in Arms

Greatly and deeply missed
my brother in arms.
Rest in peace, my friend,
a great soldier,
a great father,
a faithful and dedicated husband.
All of these things he wore so proudly
as his daily attire,
his uniform.
The lease we have on life is short.
It is unpredicted.
There is only one eternal court
who evicts out mortality.
Sadly, my comrade
has paid for someone else's sins.
Someone's selfish, irresponsible, and recklessly evil ways!
The sinner here, Al Kohall, is still alive. Unharmed even
    after murdering the innocent.
He too has relocated to walls of iron see-through bars.
Eternally, he will remain in that cell where, at the very
    least, he belongs.
Maybe, just maybe, Judge Hardaxe will have much harsher
    penalties for he who kills.
Thrill or no thrill,

was it worth the kill?
Burn you will, Al Kohall,
as the coals churn,
for SFC James Gray is smiling now
peacefully in heaven,
awaiting his family reunion.
Miss you already, my brother
Miss you already.
Peace!

Chains and Bolts

garotte
chains bolted to stone.
imprisoned I sit here in this plague-filled room
of which my next breath remain unknown.
the treachery that in this place heavily looms.
regardless of the sins that lie within two hundred rooms,
sanity or vanity,
just surviving here is insanity.
stuck between walls and metal-forged halls,
year upon year,
day upon day,
month upon month,
each day feeling more like that of a rabid beast
is my flesh what most people wish to feast.
my crime actually quite sublime,
for I did nothing more than love
her until the last blue lit chime.
innocent,
they say guilty,
as it is the truth he who prosecutes
hopes the jury never sees.
he proceeds to execute,
for I am wrongly accused.
as the upholder of the land laws

uses and abuses his power,
justice will be served.
as his drunk smile swerves his jaguar into the ditch,
the sevenfold curse of his witch is unveiled,
and the innocent now roam free.
me! finally, I am free!
as the guilty
will forever see
the lonely, dreadful
haunting of the imprisoned ghost.
may his fright
in the relentless night
give him eternal peace
as the demon who haunts
recruits him to the gauntlet militia
of the deepest fiery squadron.

Cinder Block Bay

As she sleeps through the morning darkness,
Where night had only begun,
Toward her, my soul shall run.
As the winds carry me,
The distinct sound of
gust roaring demons
In this cinder block bay.
I hear her summons
And feel our crush,
To my gothic princess I rush.

Clouds Chase the Sky

The clouds chase the sky.
These emotions for you are as endless as
the clouds above so high.
For all of my breathing life, it is you I have searched.
Now you sit perched on this lap.
An eternity I have waited
and even self-sedated on times of lonely
sobriety.
Finally, I hear you,
I see you,
I know it is you.
I know with this deranged intuition that, my mate,
I may finally meet,
for the last two met on the street
sunk their vampiric teeth into my meaty flesh.
My heart bled as these tears shed.
Now, my Gothic Princess, finally here,
for it is not money nor fame of which she adheres,
but simply the love, the natural love
that we both hold dear.
As the white clouds now chase the black from the
    blue sky,
now the bright sun sighs.

Cold Shock

Without you,
This lifeless rock
Floats without meaning
towards the vacuum-powered black hole
Days pass
As I wait in a cold shock
To hear her voice,
Even just read a text
From my one savior Princess.
Before this, black hole leaves me
Forever hexed.

Colossal Train of Coal

At a standstill in life as this
colossal train of coal
cuts me off,
my heart you stole
that night when I only wanted you to console.
I thought only of you as we kissed.
So perfect we are together
even under the worst weather.
I never in a million years dreamt our
affections would sever,
my sweet Princess.
I only ask, "What went wrong?"
I know I am masculine,
but I am not this strong.
I lie here now
in my red car.
With my ears,
I hear the metal wheels
as they squeal past me toward
my derail.

Cypress Wind

I smell the cypress wind weighing heavily on my senses,
reminding of our time so intimate
and romantic.
the trees around me so green and full of life.
lively too is our love
even through the years
and the tears.
our names remain carved
in this tree that has starved itself dry.
through all,
our hearts remain
whether through your smile and wink of an eye
or my shoulder for your head to cry.

Dancing Wind

Wind dances from left
to right
in the blackness of night,
leaves flock
to trees
like a school of birds.
This empowering emotion
strengthens
to enemies of peace,
interdependency *weakens*.

Dark Blue Gates

This darkness falls upon me.
Must now accept,
Fates bite,
And succumb to thee.
Let it be.
Let it be.
Let it be.
In this moment I pray to he.
Humbled at the dark blue gates.
I see a specter of light afar
Passing through disparage.
With fading courage,
I see the light near.
Soon,
After great pain and anguish,
Fear shall relinquish
Its hold.

Deserted Utopia

The foliage once buried now grows back.
In this utopia now deserted,
Leaves grow from concrete walls that once housed
  Earth's residents.
Playgrounds and fair rides
Desperately miss their human masters
Or playmates.
This modern-day lost community
Once thrived,
And now none can survive the
Radiant contamination
Of manmade carelessness.
Thousands have met their maker.
Thousands more grew to know helplessness,
For one simple man-made mistake has
Thrown this Europe nuclear nation into
Pandemonium.
Homes, traditions, and original cultures now lost.
That is at least a small cost of this
Twenty-four-thousand-year curse
Cast upon the innocent,
Residents of Chernobyl.
In heart and soul,
They still inhabit

Their great village.
Though they may never breathe the air of their
    home again,
For the scientific pillage forced them into
New communities,
New customs,
Newer and purer lives.
For those who are still alive,
This ordeal all should never forget
A lesson learned for a safer world
Should now be set.

Devilish Dagger

I feel your devilish Dagger
mangle my back,
splitting my spine.
this brotherly bond
of once entwined
now severed from your blade.
the judgmental thoughts
you spread like disease of me
are hard to fade,
using your stature
as a weapon to control.
I am not a child.
I have three as a matter of fact!
how defiled you callously make me feel.

Devil's Field Goal

We play on unknown murky grass
when the battle we lost at last
like the captured black sea bass.
Through the Devil's field goal, we pass.
Though our love once eternal,
now my soul so infernal.
Your smirky grin
as you kiss his chin.
My narcissistic thoughts,
now subliminal
what was once forever,
is now nevermore.
I now move on,
Creeping toward her purple sun.
Away from the pain, I now endure.
At least, the future is not as obscure
For your lure.
Be strong.
But I move on
To the purple sun
All summer long.

Delusional Sign

Her eyes pierce,
Her prance fierce.
Life of darkness,
She reigns upon
As the leaves of red
Bloom from the black trunk of pine,
Wishing to the Egyptian Isis
That one day
She will be mine.
Impatiently, I wait
The day,
The moment,
When planets align,
And our eternal union
Is more than just a delusional sign.

Eternal Sunrise

her voice screams loudly
my name.
I look sharply to the left
then to the right,
up,
down,
all around.
no one but myself
but her voice as if she were
next to me.
the word "what!" I slur,
for it is but a blur.
for years she haunts.
this voice unexpectedly daunts
as I sleep.
she cries
at times
she resides in dreams.
her black hair and blue eyes,
her seductive voice,
and sweet loving guise.
is she friend or foe?
is she to be my demise
or the beginning of eternal sunrise?

Evil Boar

pleasantly receive the stones and the sticks
you bring as I hear your
love blitz.
I expect it was no more than my normal goth clutz self.
your book lie upon my shelf
your love I wish only for
myself.
bear my heart to you as you bear yours,
and together we will ward off evil boars.

Evil Nazi

forced by the evil Nazi to let my
gothic princess go
as I starve in these wet, cold
electronically
poisoning fences.
the speakers all round display the sorrowful sound
as deeper my frown for awaiting tomorrow grow,
watching now the archaic reaper sow
seeds of plague,
and still I pray for your last saving breath upon these cold
    blue lips.
my eyes now lined with a saggy black,
wishing that your love was back.
Eternally, I reside here in this modern-day Dachau
with only your past ghost beside me
until finally, all dismay
may be dismissed,
and resting souls have found eternal bliss.

Evil Warrior

what a way to start this day.
just one small stretch until the end of today.
this selfless servant makes one last stop on his way home
to start his day with his family.
in their soft, loving sheets, his children lay,
awaiting their hero,
anxious to play.
She waits also for her hubby
to tell her all is okay.

Floodgates

open up the floodgates, and let the salty beast roar
as the rashing, lesionous cold sore
infects the razorblade boar,
for she who spreads disease
with the spraying of bees knees,
with her succulent breeze.
for what seems as pleasant as a harvest and his peasant
is likely to be the tainted
permanently painted scars.
hail to guardian of the ocean
flood the evildoers from this heart.
abolish the cultivated hate,
mend these wounds,
and secure my fate.

Gold Linings

As he thieves the goods from the neighbor's home,
He believes himself the master of his art.
As he attempts to deceive,
The torrent shatters the back room glass to rashly leave.
The goods he gathered
shall lather his pocket with lush gold linings.
Though his neighbor
spent many years of labor to enjoy these
gifts of grandeur,
now, after many years of hard work to pay for
    these rewards,
within a second, they have vanished
by the hands of a one too lazy to lift a hand to help one in
    need
but anxious to help feed his own greed.
This seed he has grown so many years ago
stems from a deeper addiction,
an affliction that may soon kill
but will definitely find a new home:
an eight-by-eight cell.
Was it worth the merch you stole?
You are only a doll now between iron bars
perched for all to watch you fall.

Heart Falls

She ignores my calls,
my every whimper,
as this heart falls.
Isn't it enough that my soul
I sold to her?
In your presence, I fold,
remembering her soft skin.
As we hold each other tightly,
I think of you nightly.
Nancy, don't leave me
anything you ask.
I will make my number 1 task
but please, Nancy, don't flee on me now.
Thinking of the times we lay in the dark,
lost in our eyes and thoughts,
waiting on the neighbor's dog to bark,
now I am alone in the dark.

Heaven Smile

looking at her heavenly smile
saddens me beyond the most vile.
running through dark shadows
in the night valley,
I hear the whisper of my twenty-one volleys
and the toll keeper
collecting tokens for his trolley.
Redemption draws near,
but the lengthy cost of what is left of this heart
is what I fear.
I wonder if it is me she hears
as her lucid eyes sleep.
Howl of the Lycan
the wolves howl in victory
at the fowl now devoured
under the full-lit moon.
as his vampire lays strewn,
this curse explodes like the black balloon.
volatile, his heart races,
only wanting a life
a life with slow pace.
the wolves howl at the break of witching hour,
for this is when the curse will devour
his heart, though, far from sour

her face always in his mind.
anxiously, his lycan mind wants the
clouds to blanket and warm the demonic full moon.
by the fire, she remains,
waiting for her loving, but howling, lycan,
awaiting, the glorious union of her man.

Involuntarily Submissive

life force from my mind and body drained as I look upon
abundant fresh green maples
of which are freshly rained.
the staples pierce deep
as I now am involuntarily submissive to
the harsh elements of life
driving down the pitch-black road
awaiting the daisy chain of events to explode.

Jacqueline Frost

I support your dependent need for affection,
investing the cost of my life, blood, and soul
with all this heartache I invest,
yet, still, you rip this heart from my chest.
I only asked for your love.
I stare at the sky above
and see the geese flying south
In a formal wedge formation,
avoiding inflammation and
escaping the wrath of the fierce
Jacqueline Frost,
whistling her winds of cold-heartedness,
for it is all at the cost of his heart, not hers.
All I ever wanted
was to sync your mouth to mine
so that our souls would entwine.
Now I await the hearse for this heart,
my soul, however, callous and strong
as geese who have now reached
their stronghold without breach
as they secure their mountaintop at all 360 degrees.
Though your thoughts are evil enough to cybergenically
    freeze,
Camp Geese in the tropical south will melt all of

your cold evil spells.
On this Beach, I lie with no more thoughts of you
knowing that my security cannot
and will not be breached. At least by you!
Here I lie in my tropical paradise,
which has melted your ice cold into the deep sea.

Key to My Soul

Thee who hold
The key
To my soul
Is the one
With control.
There is only
One whom I allow
Power over me,
And that is me,
Only me,
So mote it be.

Kindred Spirit

Kindred your spirit
With such impervious wit
As you knit my heart into design
Of your fit.
I lay disembodied as you mold me into your creature.
Somber the soul as I must transform
In order to calm your storm,
As I prepare my true heart for the fall,
The great plunge down the infamous chute.
Just the other side that wall,
Her black shadow paces the hall.
So mysteriously elegant she does enthrall.
Curiously numb to my pains,
It is in this moment she reigns.
Heart beats erratic
As I feel her energy static.
My mind racing frantic
As I stare at my doppelganger after lethargic decades pass.
I recall my deep love for her black shadow,
The love that kills
Is found at Waverly Hills.

King of Evil

As the spring blooms
Of colors bright,
Loom over the perfect green grass,
And the sun peaks his head out from the dark, dank
    clouds of a ten-year winter,
Joy consumes all around the globe,
Thrilled that, finally, the king of evil on earth
Has been annihilated.
I lay here on this sofa completely elated,
Knowing that finally, the skies are no longer gray.
On this day,
He, the King of Terror, is at the bottom of the
    Arabian sea.
His corpse lay wrapped in white,
Sleeping with the fish of the sea
Until they take their last bite of his flesh.
Good-bye, terrorist king.

Love and Despair

the days we share
and promised to eternally care
somehow end as rash
as our sudden union.
love turns to despair,
for one or both promisors
have lost interest in contracts,
wishing maybe that the other end of this portal
shall provide
life anew,
but this portal is one endless black hole
where the destination cannot be seen
nor measured.
can these flames not be reflared?
light the orange-red flameless burning logs
with the most expensive petrol,
and with this, the partner you once slaved to pleasure
may close the endless black hole of no measure.

Love Resides

I feel her presence beside me.
Her pleasant love
Resides in my core
Even in her absence.
Our pain, we share.
Our eternal love
Will never tear,
For he who shall interfere,
Prepare for the loneliness you shall wear.

Loving Hiss

As I miss
Her loving hiss,
Memories serve
As temporary sanity
And bliss.
I recall the horrors of one May's eve
When ice cold pierced my heart.
All I dreamt of was her kiss.
Now her kiss is all I have
When there was a time
That her kiss was all of who I…

Lucifina

as my actions of yesterday
haunt me this 666th day of the week,
I thought escaping emotions would be
simple and sleek,
but now, I found myself at the point of those most weak,
for though I thought you to be Lucifina then.
I was surely the most Evil for eluding
my love,
to you, my love,
my Lucifina...
may I be your eternal.
I dream only of our devilish romance
gain another chance.
for at retro glance,
mistakes seem clearer.
I pray my Lucifina
deems me worthy
and spare me from lashes
and ashes.
I love her,
always have.
only my ignorance
and momentary pestilence
blew out our Franken scents,

our eternal love fragrance.
forgive me, I plea.
looking in your eyes,
our blissful forever, I dream.

Mannequin Mausoleum

Lying here in this cubbyhole tomb
where we await
our mandated doom
from our wish master,
our names, replaced with numbers
on our cubby in front of our plastic-hardened heads,
our Freedom sacrificed so all others
may safely rest their heads.
I hear her voice in the distance.
She faded from me decades ago.
I left her
only to protect her.
Now, two decades later,
this sweet voice of liberty
rains down on this mannequin mausoleum.
number replaced with name.
all given up without shame
now, at last,
Freedom reigns!

Melting Stone Hills

Emotions cause these rash commotions,
making my mind spiral uncontrollably,
traveling to a destination called sweet inferno,
reaching and yelping for
help!
No reply!
Destiny unknown.
Deep in these coals, I am thrown
from green grass and yellow daffodils
to fiery red coals
and melting stone hills,
but yet, here I am plummeting,
and still, I float downward, praying,
saying,
"God help me!"

Mesmerize

In this moment, I lay mesmerized,
Mesmerized by your touch,
Your loving caress,
Dreaming of you, my sweet angel,
My crutch,
My fix.
You are the clutch that drives this machine forward.
Our meeting I always look toward.
My sweet black-haired princess
Is the driving force
That keeps me on the right course.
You are my rails to this train

Misconstrue

The caring, loving, and
selfless you,
I would take in by two,
or was it all a façade.
I grew to misconstrue
all in my aura.
I felt you were true,
agonized at the words:
"We are through."
If I could apologize and wipe
the black hole away,
then an apology times ten
for you I would give
and promise to never
from your side stray.

Mortality Gates

Her sweet voice,
In her absence, I miss.
Separated from her,
Not by choice.
Patiently,
For I wait in this
Lonely stone cell
For her kiss
To free me from this personal hell.
This ring of black diamond awaits
My gothic princess.
Eternally, we shall remain
Even beyond mortality gates.

Muster

Searching diligently
for your gorgeous green hair,
these eyes see deep
behind the wall that shields her mind.
With this love-lust,
one is sure to go blind
even as you snare.
I can only submissively stare
as she cast her spell.
Yellow fog of muster gas
fills this air I breathe.
I care not as
my mask lends me protection,
and it is thee
that I still see
through the poisonous, colorful breeze
to our shelter I go
where I shall prepare our eternal
candlelit date,
for it is us together, alas

My Atomic Fallout

Picking up the
debris flurrying
about
from my atomic
fallout,
thinking of the
times we shared,
so many thoughts once seemed pleasant,
even comforting.
Was this only a fling
or less than even just a thing?
I bleed out all my emotions,
lay all cards on the table for you.
How defiled I now feel.
I see our destruction
like a fluorescent green-mushroomed flame
spreading faster than
nuclear epidemic.
Am I to blame,
or is it you that need be ashamed?
Against my will, you set me free.
For you, it was only your vanity (and fame)
which brought you concern.

Mystic Heiress

My Princess
Of silk red-black hair, I miss.
Every second,
Every minute,
Of separation
Hurts like the bite
Of the rattlesnake's hiss.
Her voice I hear play
In this head.
Her pain I feel as if I were
To be fillet.
Miles may bring distance,
But our bond grows a stronghold through
Resistance.
My mystic heiress of this heart,
Forever only briefly describes us.

North Star

As I look upon the North star
that makes herself known from afar,
thoughts gaze
to our former flame ablaze.
Mistakes of yesterday,
I now pay for today.
My life now, without you, disarray,
actually, more like dismay.
You always gave me your light, your ray.
Now, it is my fault
that our bond be eternally forgotten in this ice-cold vault.
You I will forever exalt.

Nurse of the Beast

Mortuary smells of dead coal
from the maze of mines below.
As her plague genuflects before him,
he does not detect what is to come.
His feelings are too certain,
her intent for him is
vague at best.
Soon, his heart will sag
like his hammock on a lazy summer day
as her tail wags,
and she displays her magical sway.
This breed of black cat
with her black zombified eyes,
some have named her the nurse of the beast,
for the man of the night is her feast.
She draws his blood with her fangs
and her sharp sinful paws,
and all he hears is her sweet, sweet *meow*.
Enticed, he stays
curious as the cat herself he lay in this nest.
Heart now slashed in two.
Love now dead.
There is no cure,
for her bite is forever infectious.

Nyctanthous

I dream of sleep
as I lie here, I weep,
for thee I so love and already miss.
This black rose lays upon the mantle
In hopes that what we have shall never
be dismantled.
I work so hard to impress
and be sure to give you all needed to decompress
even if the cost is the severing of my heart.
Lucky be the man who holds your pureness.
Such as the black rose has profound qualities,
so too is your passion,
so nyctanthous.
Your fangs as sharp as panthers.
Our lips locked as soft as
hydrangeas.

Phased Love

Was our love only a phase for you?
I spill my heart to thee,
And yet again silent you flee.
I pour my affection full into thou chalice
Only for your rejection and malice.
I bury myself in this self-dug grave
With only you to crave.
Fighting to be free of your shackles,
If only I could be so brave.
Dreams of leaving your hassles
Lie upon these frayed tassels.

Queen of the Peach State

This beauty and love that you naturally hold so true
Is so much so
That even the royals must commit in the Abbey.
Your beauty *greatly* surpasses all.
You more royal than thee!
For you are the Genuine Queen of all pure
And divine
Like the priceless and everlasting love
Of our Prince and Princess, William and Kate.
So too is your colossal loving heart.
Happiness was your fate.
Now finding that special one,
Your smile and natural happiness
Become an addiction I must crave.
For companions and smiles
Have not exactly been
In abundance in me lately
seeing that everlasting, upside-down frown
makes me want such even more.
She is out there,
well, somewhere…
One day we will meet
and be as happy as the Queen of the Peach State.
Hail to my Queen.

Rest Haven

You say you miss me,
But do you, really?
When you are not by my side
I feel an eternal void.
I ask for you to be closer
And save my soul from foreclosure.
Your response
Colder than one icy night in Siberia!
Sorry if love is not a part of your criteria.
What we once had,
It's done
Laying forever in eternal rest haven.

Roller Coaster

Our love like a roller coaster,
Riding with you through thick
And through thin,
Remaining to defend your sin.
Here I stay for you,
The stain of your love.
Never shall I abstain
Though brutally slain
As plummet down to Earth.
By your side, I stay in your domain

Rugged Disguise

I hear our chime of gothic romance
And look at my android to have a glance.
And then I see
It has been you all my life,
The one of which I have dreamt of
Since birth.
We are destined to meet on this earth.
Each day, I see your hand reach to save me.
I can't help but stare deep into thine eyes.
Behind my rugged disguise,
I really need you to save me from demise.

Serpent Eel

For those who hate or discriminate,
I say to you,
This day,
Thank you,
Thank you for your
Gift to amuse and entertain
Though it looks from up here that you are struggling with
    rough terrain down there.
For those who steal
Or attempt to steal,
Enjoy your feast of veal,
For
Before your very eyes,
It shall turn to
Serpent eel,
For your heart is not real,
And your soul in Hades will
Eternally feel.

Sheathed Knife

He who discriminates against me,
my way of life,
my provisions for my circular family,
I kindly, first, ask that you leave your knife sheathed.
I would much prefer not to feel a red-pierced stab in my
    back
by your brutal attack of my innocent life.
I, for sure,
would not condemn thee
on your land where you roam free
with no need for security.
After several years past,
I ask why it is
that this spell upon me you cast.
Guilty, I do plea,
guilty for sacrificing
and providing
for my Family.

Siberian Fur

I would drop all for her
Without one single slur,
Rushing toward the warmth
Of her jacket of Siberian fur.
Her smile comforts me.
Her touch converts me
From old ways.
Her kiss
As calm as the blue Caribbean Sea.

Slurpy

I thought we had something special
though not normal,
at least by standards of society,
but it's evident that,
my heart,
you are not worthy,
at least what is left
of the slurpy
mess you made of it.

Soiled Dove

save me from my self-destruct
as I lay the adhesive duct upon
the red detonation cord.
for our eternity, I was hoping we would permanently
    construct.
I find I am nothing more to you than the wood
that was placed in our fireplace just now.
carefully, I navigate when I speak,
for one wrong tweak of words
may provoke the morbidity
I so long to not seek.
though I love her eternal,
this pain,
this torture,
I can no longer nurture
my soiled dove
I so love.
if only she felt the same for me,
maybe the shame
would not be as easy to see.
my soiled dove,
I pray for her eternal love.

Soul Soother

You have single-handedly melted the icicles
That for years have bound this heart,
Saving my soul from
Inevitable agony.
How can your touch upon my face
Warm my heart and soul
And make the past hurt erase?
Every waking second,
I now can only think of you.
When I am cross,
You ground me.
When I am saddened,
You lift me up.
When I am hurting, you shield me

The Staircase

Your ghost floats toward me
from above,
asking why I have
abandoned
from the staircase below.
I sit in pain,
agony,
fear,
as I gauze my wound upon my pale white skin.
Your sweet, loving voice
Sedates,
not sure to what in my life this relates.
Is your haunting the end of my mortal fates
or a warning
to heed or ignore by choice?
Her voice,
oh that sweet, caressing voice,
"Why are you leaving me!?"
she says,
Why are you leaving me?"
As I whimper and stare into empty eyes,
my heart impaled,
my soul severed.

Starling

In your absence,
I lose persistence.
I stare at the black notebook that lies
in the middle of my beige floor,
challenging me
as salt-watered eyes
rapidly form a river flowing down my chest,
gushing out the memories
of yesterday.
As Hindemith talks to me in his orchestral tone,
my throne of blue, I sit in,
thinking only of your
memories fond and sweet,
not bad ones, only good.
She was a camouflaged Angel,
always putting all before her,
placing herself last.
It is her good-heartedness
and love that I gratefully received.
When I lost belief,
when I may have lost faith,
there was that Angel.
The times I felt hopeless,
the time I felt careless,

there was that Angel,
elegantly dressed in battle fatigue,
killing the sinful things that once haunted my thoughts
disguised in digital camouflage
with her perplexing smile and
comforting hug
that lifted my spirit
and saved me from being scathed.
Missed immensely
though her presence on this plain lost,
Solace has been found.
As you now sit on the throne of winged saviors
who you peacefully command
with perfect love in your heart,
I look upon the clouds
as if they are your shrouds,
for I know Stephanie is always there
when in need.

Tears These Eyes Expel

As the tyrant of this soul throws the wind across the land,
the tears that these eyes expel
fly like floating sprinkles from one end of the globe to
    the next.
It is you I hoped I could repel,
for your soul is now up for sale
in my garage.
Enough of the abuse,
for I am not a recluse.
The mortar barrage you throw,
I shall no longer sow,
so this is where I tell you
to go!
Go back to the storms that you
so craftly brew
but that you shall do
for someone else's blood be strewn

Termite Queen

Bullying
both mental
as well as
physical
as you attempt your flawful
and, need I say,
predictable
attack,
it is me who has the laugh in the end,
for as you dream only of profit,
the great and knowledgeable prophet
sees your future.
As you send your termite militia,
the nuclear chemical will
terminate thee,
leaving your lonely soul
screaming in the deep inferno
yet yearning for content.
Cut me off from my path,
and I walk over you like a speed bump, I promise.
You do the math,
an eternal friendship
or an eternal hell?
Your choice.

The Stabbing

We see the same vision—unity between two hearts—then you violently stab deep past the flesh. Now I wish I took a cab from your tomb, for you were the venom for years I fear, your cries I hear. My soul, the judge, sentences thee to eternal guillotine just as that of Constantine.

Torrential Tears

I sleep
Or
Attempt to count sheep,
But then, every corner
I see her.
Anxiously, I awake
Only to find my eyes made a mistake.
Her love in her absence,
I feel
As strong as the harshest forged steel.
Her black hair
Curls within. Every fiber of thought
In my solitude,
I see her.
In my soul, I feel her.
Without her here,
All is just a blur.
Only wish
I could have her,
My gothic princess.
As she smiles,
I smile for her,
While my mistakes from our past drench me in torrential
Salt tears.

Unexpected Propensity

you have been my life
for as long as this eternal steel knife.
I always dreamt you shall be my wife,
but then, my dark evil opponent
appears with unexpected propensity.
maybe
I should be sad or defeated,
but
hell no!
my heartbreak will never be repeated.
from you, I set myself free.
my once-crowned gothic princess,
I shall now crown another worthy heiress.
my heart will continually chime,
for it is now her time,
as yours is now over.

Until I Am Blind

The hurt you bring
When you sing
Tears through this body
As brisk as the ice-cold spring,
I relinquished all
For your tribute,
Your splendor
Is my heart enslaved,
And yet, I continue,
Struggling to stay in the high tides of
Your wave.
Escape crosses the mind,
But her current sucks me under.
My hands now wrinkled,
My shoulders now shivering,
My mind fears what is near,
My toes now a soothing numb
As she sucks the soul out of me.

Veins of Light Blue

When one
Manipulates
This heart she decapitates,
Warmness once flowed through
These veins of light blue.
Now the stream turns a
Solid, frigid cold.
Once love prevalent,
Now, the thought
Distant.

Viola

You will be missed
With great times together reminisced.
Whether work or play,
These dimples bloom, a joyful display.
Separated by unending miles,
Your picture everyday in these files of thoughts.
Though far away by man-made measure,
Our hearts are as close together.
As the maestro and his meticulous orchestra,
So sweet the sound of "The Walton" comes from his
    crafty viola;
asserting a bond so strong, even distance cannot part.

Volatile Cloudiness

As the clouds somber in shade to volatile,
My mood shifts from content to hostile.
Why?
Why does this heart,
This soul,
This mind,
Experience so much suffrage.
Why don't you just mix me in to your boiling pot of
    porridge
Such as the witch with the house of bread and ginger and
    sugar?
You lure your prey
With a sweet, simple, and innocent, high-pitched "Hey."
Then with a simple smile
And wink,
All submit to thee.
Your game, we unknowingly play
Until you are done.
Then, for us, it is dismay.
At least, before our involuntary self-destruct,
We see one last time
That beautiful smile
And radiant blonde flowing hair,
For which once it was happiness we did share.

White Arctic Shadow

Rustling through the white shadows that fall lightly from
    above without stall,
From the nocturnal clouds that stare down on me,
Heart grows to a fierce arctic level
As you near me;
Wind as stabbing as thine dagger,
Air turning these cheeks to a blood-red,
Too bad you could not have brought me warmth, instead
Reaching out to someone,
Anyone!
Please stop these bleeds!
This heart needs the warmth of the Caribbean,
Not the frigidity of your jealous hate!
When you are near
My cold insanity, I fear.
So there it is, I shall always persevere
No matter how harsh the winter wind!
Those who want to show aggression toward me,
Whether from hate, fear, or jealousy,
I am here waiting.
Your destiny, we shall see,
Ice-pierced heart now melting
As the avalanche flows gently now to the

Peaceful shore,
Where the pirates of yesterday
Have ceased to exist.

Captivated

Captivated by your deep-black eyes and yellow hair,
Here I stand!
Entranced, I remain and can only stare in awe,
For within your essence, I find no flaw.
Your breathtaking beauty lures me to you
Without warning.
My senses, unconscious by your venomous bite.
As you have me in your sight,
I draw near to my woman of perfection,
longing for your touch and everlasting infection.
As your poisonous love runs through my veins,
Wishing only our future without pains
In deep hope of remaining love with no stains,
Though different we may be,
It is our love that all will see.

Elegant Witch

The elegant witch casts her spell,
This curse though, not from Hell.
It is her delicate touch I feel from the ring of the bell.
In an instant, it is I who fell.
As the knees weaken,
I see the beacon of her love.
Now comes the black dove,
Perching his claws into me.
As the light suddenly shine above,
I grab hold to her soft, comforting arms,
Accepting all of her charms.
And aloft we travel.
With eternal affection, we shalt not be led astray.
True love may temporarily fray,
But it is with our soul mate whom with we stay.

Gray Bird

The day starts as normal as the other,
Bright sunny day with the birds peacefully chirping.
Then, with no warning,
The annoying creature beside me rings, rings, rings
As loud as the holocaust horn.
When answering the phone, I hear Officer on the other
    end sing my name.
This call made my fatherly heart fall,
Notified that I must leave my life,
Vacate in order to defend is now my strife.
Though no wife to leave behind,
I have my son to tend,
Not knowing what may be across the bend.
I board this gray bird to ascend thirty thousand feet,
The sky now turning gray and dreary.
My stomach feels eerie,
Knowing the flags of my new residence
Rot, Grun, und Schwartz,
Knowing, though, that this service will save the worlds
    from evil.
I take solace in stopping the upheaval.
Forlorn I leave my firstborn
For a short time.

Hydrangea's of Black and Purple

The hydrangeas of black and purple
Dehydrated by the infamous sun
Scorching down upon them
With their end in clear sight;
Love so perfect
As this season ends, the loving plants
Genuflect,
Giving way for the frigid cold white layering
The colorful garden of life;
The large friend the maple has surrendered her leaves,
They feel the frostbitten air
Taking them to eternal sleep
As they wilt toward one another,
One last eternal kiss of love
They give without a scare
Fear not death when love is in thine heart
For love so true
Is indeed a Love Eternal.

Jagged Mountaintop

As I sit on this jagged mountaintop looking down upon
The ragged river that flows below,
Thoughts of my life and the past are bestowed upon me,
Things that stab like a knife at the very spirit within;
The natural innocence of the rolling stream
Acknowledges the sin I carry.
This sin to be buried deep within the granite stone I
    lean upon;
Tomorrow, it will be but a dream.
With much weight lifted from my heart,
I can now have a new start;
Sitting on this mountaintop in search for
Clarity,
The one Divine, I finally see
A great beginning bequeaths me
After years of being blind.

My Hell

Why do I remain in this cell you gave me!
It is my Hell.
Your love, once Heavenly,
Now a life sentence in this jail.
My soul, because of you, so frail.
Where did the one I love go?
Or was that all just one big show?
You changed from shielding me from my foes
That from the rapids below my feet flow
To throwing me to the sharks
That violently bark for new flesh.
So why! Why have you ground my heart into this mesh?
I loved you with all my soul,
And when I thought you loved me,
You left me to decompose and rot.
You, who once claimed me as a prized possession,
Now nothing more than an obsession,
An object,
An object you can control.
Well, control me no more;
On this day, I take flight.
The fear of insecurity and reprisal
Is no more.

Frederick Jones

I shall shed no more tears for your loss
You, to me now, are no more than the decay from my
    teeth I floss.

Peace Soft as Fleece

Peace as soft as fleece,
Tranquil rest my knees
In this time of needs;
Taken with despair
Over the loss of one for whom I care.
Serenity consumes me,
Knowing my friend is amongst Angels
Watching over us from all angles.
Pain he no longer knows,
Thinking of him as I hear the banner spangled.
Missing him, my eyes water,
As he is my Grandfather
There for me in life.
Here for me now, in spirit and memory.

Leave Me Hangin'

As you leave me hangin'
Like a rack of ribs
In the Butcher's smoke room
Just waiting to be dropped in the Witches' cauldron,
Your cruelty, I can take no longer,
Feeling this noose grip tightly round my neck;
As you kick the surface below me,
It is your accusations I hang for,
So quick to persecute!
Casting judgment upon me!
Who are you to judge this soul?
Who are you to allege my intent?
As my toes wiggle on the chair you have propped
    below me,
I watch the evil in your grin rise;
Despair, much to your surprise,
I will not succumb to,
Free from your evil eternally;
This warlock guards the steeple
To keep away your devilish ways,
You claim to be that of God.
Yet your actions are quite the contrary;
Different in my ways and values I may be
To thee,

But the same nonetheless.
I too love,
I too loathe,
I also, like you, envy.
We both love to smile.
So how different am I
That you smile when I die
A warlock is what you accuse me of?
When all I am is free to speak,
Free to be who I am,
Free to be me
Though different than most,
I am free to be who I may,
And here you stand to threaten my freedom;
Hang me if you so choose.
My soul will last much longer than your booze,
And haunt you eternally this murdered soul
Shall
For now, I am free from judgment.
I am free to do what thou wilt,
Abbrahadabra!

Queen of Shebah

As she slithers her way into my aura,
Paralyzed I must lay in this coffin;
Her venom injected into these veins
Leaving the eternal, morbid stains
Of her snakebite upon my neck;
Her cunning eyes entrap
I can only glare at her as I hear her snare;
Then comes her mantra!
As She, the Queen of Shebah, controls
All of her prey like helpless trolls,
Should I free myself?
Or should I stay? Fearing I may harm her emotions;
Stay for a while longer I must.
But one more time! One more time!
One more outburst of evil insanities,
And I am out!
Then it happens yet again,
and another for the thousandth time,
and yet I have learned nothing!
For here, I lie,
Taking the abuse,
But now, I am ready to oppose her
As she moves in for her venomous kiss;
I strike back silently

And dreadfully as that of the Brown Recluse,
Not so painful,
At least at first,
But decays the flesh as the venom spreads
Paralyzing,
Until she can no longer advance toward me!
With this, we are finally through,
Over and done with,
And now moving on to enjoy the pleasantries of life.

Special Thanks

Thank you most importantly to all fans, friends, and family for your continued support!